AF881040

What Our Readers Have Said...

"Although I consider myself a seasoned sales professional, it is helpful to have past learning's refreshed. The books were also beneficial because of the information concerning 'trends' in the sales relationship. The sales process should be viewed as dynamic since business relationships change regularly."

•

"For the particular business I am in and the type of sales calls I have, I find that the books in the Pinpoint Sales Training Series are very often applicable to how I conduct business. I would recommend them to other sales people, just not ones that are in my industry."

•

"These books provide very good concepts. It fits in well with the Bell Leadership training program that I attended in November."

•

"I use this material in these books and apply it to my customers and other employees I work with."

•

"I would like to know other topics. Is there anything on Production Management or Consultative Selling or Time Management?"

•

"These books are great tools that should be used as guidelines for our everyday

supervisory practices. You need to take the time to do a short self-evaluation when reading them."

•

"The Pinpoint Training Series delivers information that could be used in a lot different areas."

•

"I like this because I can take them with me to read at a convenient time. I feel the little time I have to spend in the office is best use on activities that directly relate to revenue opportunities. I like the short amount of time it takes to keep up with these."

•

"I prefer the self-study approach; it fits in with my schedule."

•

"My thought is that the real value of these books comes into effect when doing the action plans."

•

"Short and sweet. These books are easy to comprehend."

•

"I have enjoyed reading these books. They are relevant to today's work environment and the ongoing change in the way we manage our workforce."

•

"I do feel that these books have been very helpful to me at my job."

•

"I think a lot of the recommendations in these books are very useful, and can be applicable to everyday situations. If nothing else, it's a good reference guide to fall back upon if a situation arises in the future."

•

"These books are relevant to today's work environment and the ongoing change in the way we manage our workforce."

•

Productive Sales Networking

Pinpoint Sales Skill Development Training Series

TIMOTHY F. BEDNARZ

MAJORIUM
BUSINESS PRESS

Pinpoint Sales Skill Development Training Series
"Productive Sales Networking"
Timothy F. Bednarz

Graphic design: Monika Pawlak

Majorium Business Press
2025 Main Street
Stevens Point, WI 54481
715.342.1018 • 800.654.4935

ISBN 978-1-882181-90-2

Printed in the United States of America

Introduction

The Pinpoint Sales Skill Development Training Series is designed for targeted training and education regarding increased improvement in a specific skill or competency.

Each book within this series is designed to be easy to use, understand and apply to your job. It can be used as a basis for training individuals, as a discussion guide or as a personal training tool.

Each chapter within this book discusses a specific concept. When you have completed all eight chapters you should have a 360° perspective of the topic.

Additionally, each chapter is divided into specific sections:

- The first section provides you with an overview of the topic
- The Implications section discusses why the concept is important, and why it is important to learn and apply.
- The Strategies, Tips & Techniques to Apply section teaches how to use and apply the particular concept to your work.
- The Points to Ponder section gives you something to think about or to be discussed with a group setting. These are questions not meant to be immediately answered, but to be pondered over time.
- The Training Activity section provides you with the tools to transfer what you have learned to your job. It is designed to help create an action plan to effectively apply the concept.

Each of the topics in this series is time-tested and proven in the marketplace. They have been used by thousands of employees as training tools. Many of the users have commented that what made these books valuable, was the ability to refer to them when a problem surfaced. They indicated that they remembered reading about the exact problem. They referred back to these books and found an appropriate solution.

You will find them equally valuable as a resource in your professional development library.

Table of Contents

1. Why Networking Is an Essential Sales Skill 1

2. Factors That Impact Networking 5

3. What Salespeople Can Expect from Networking 9

4. The Ineffective Networker 13

5. Problems and Pitfalls Associated with Networking 17

6. The Best Networking Practices 21

7. Developing a Networking Strategy 25

8. Tracking Your Network 29

LEARNING OBJECTIVES:

- To understand the elements of networking.
- To apply effective networking techniques.
- To develop effective network contacts.
- To develop a proper networking protocol.
- To avoid common problems and pitfalls associated with networking.

1

Why Networking Is an Essential Sales Skill

Buyers make decisions based upon trust. Every buying decision is a leap of faith on their part: they trust the representations made by both the company and the salesperson that the product or service will do what they both say it will do. Once a buyer trusts the salesperson, they will have sufficient confidence to refer him or her to a friend or associate.

IMPLICATIONS – WHAT THIS MEANS TO YOU

Networking should be an important consideration and an essential sales skill for every salesperson. Research has shown that 60% to 80% of referred leads buy, and in fewer sales calls. Additionally, referred leads are four times more likely than any other prospect to refer the salesperson to another prospective customer.

This is important for salespeople to understand because personal relationships and business relationships are intertwined. Many salespeople resist the idea of asking happy customers and friends for referrals, somehow feeling it is degrading to cultivate personal relationships. The reality is that every salesperson needs a support system.

STRATEGIES, TIPS & TECHNIQUES TO APPLY

Networking is effective because trust and compatibility are important in relationships. People tend to build closer relationships with people who think like they do. The maxim, "It's not what you know, but who you know," is very close to reality.

In any salesperson's world, there are people in a position to influence their success. They have the ability to mentor and coach the salesperson, and provide him or her with access to important resources, contacts and information. Often all the salesperson has to do is ask for the help.

While the concept of networking creates a perception that it focuses one's efforts on external sources, salespeople should not forget to network internally with individuals in their own company. Research has consistently found that one of the key factors that separate top from average sales performers is the ability to gain the cooperation of their own support staff on behalf of their customers.

Additionally, as salespeople work with major accounts, they "rub elbows" with numerous individuals. While many may be directly involved and others just advising, the development of each of these individuals provides salespeople with a number of potential referral resources.

The key in networking is to develop a strategy that helps salespeople identify individuals who are in the position to act as influencers. These may include people who are already referring salespeople to other prospects or others who may be in the position to refer them in the future. When a salesperson establishes a relationship with a contact, both parties should be able to help each other out. In this fashion, salespeople are wisely investing their time in sustainable relationships. Going beyond mere acquaintance, such relationships are built on mutual trust and rapport. If salespeople have selected the right influencers, they will discover that 10 to 20% will provide them with 80% of referrals.

Salespeople must also understand that many people want to help them with a referral, but these individuals may feel an offer of assistance will be insulting. Consequently, it is important that salespeople ask directly for help, perhaps in the form of advice, and then for referrals to other buyers they may know that could benefit from the same level of service provided to them. Often these customers will be delighted to be of assistance and even flattered that the salesperson thought enough to ask them.

Salespeople often think networking is limited to outside activities and events. While these are useful in identifying potential contacts for future development, many will find that the best source of networked referrals are customers they already know, who like them and are happy to provide additional contacts for them to potentially sell to. If the salesperson is reliable and makes the referral source look good, then they will be a sustainable source of new business.

POINTS TO PONDER — SOMETHING TO THINK ABOUT

1. How often do you foster relationships with customers to the point they can be helpful as referral sources?
2. Are you afraid to ask customers for referrals or do you routinely do it?

TRAINING ACTIVITY — APPLICATION & ACTION PLAN

1. Review your account files and identify your best possible referral sources.
2. Identify how they can specifically help you.
3. Identify how you can specifically help them.
4. Prioritize your list and identify the best possibilities.
5. Determine how you can begin to foster and nurture these relationships.

2

Factors That Impact Networking

While networking is a common term bandied about in sales and during sales training, it is not something that a salesperson just does. It takes planning, persistence and commitment toward a long-term goal. Part of the salesperson's lifestyle, it begins with a foundation of trust that must first be earned before any benefits can be derived from it.

IMPLICATIONS – WHAT THIS MEANS TO YOU

People buy from people they like. This is an old adage in sales. While many of the changes and restructurings in the corporate world have destroyed many sales relationships over the years and minimized the amount of time a buyer can devote to a salesperson, that adage is still as true today as it was years ago. Not only do people buy from people they like, but they also want to see them succeed. This is the essence of successful networking: the ability of salespeople to work with people who like them and want to help them succeed.

Effective networking is built first and foremost on the foundation of trust, shared interests and mutual friendship. When these factors are firmly established, salespeople will see their investment in relationships flourish.

STRATEGIES, TIPS & TECHNIQUES TO APPLY

A successful, sustainable and comprehensive networking program is not developed overnight, and, as such, should be a long-range goal. Referrals can in fact be gained through the immediate implementation of a networking plan, but the ultimate gains and returns are developed through planned and sustained efforts. The factors salespeople should consider that impact effective and successful networking include:

Trust

Effective networking demands that all relationships be built upon mutual trust. Novice salespeople are often seen eagerly "working the room" at an event or association meeting, attempting to secure referrals and contacts. Their actions are often amateurish and transparent. The "what's in it for me" comes across so strongly as to render their efforts counterproductive. All too often, eager networkers demand referrals without bringing anything of value to the table for the other party. Trust is replaced by a perception of greed.

Effective networkers carefully select either individuals who they have had previous business dealings with or prospects who may benefit from their products or services in the future. They build both a business and personal relationship with these individuals. Their motivation is not to use these people but to work with them. Salespeople must typically invest a great deal of time and energy establishing and nurturing these relationships before they see a substantial return from their efforts. However, trust and rapport take time to establish, and until these are firmly rooted in the relationship, it will be premature to push for referrals. Most salespeople have a number of such relationships firmly established. These should be the starting point for their network.

Attitude

Salespeople must have the right attitude in order to sustain quality networking relationships. In most cases where successful relationships are established, the attitude is one of friendship and a mutual desire to help one's friends. There is a natural give and take to the relationship and a mutual desire to see one another succeed. This is always a preferable place to start any networking relationship.

In cases where friendship has yet to be established, salespeople should develop a service attitude. This demonstrates that their motivation is to help the other party, either as a friend, associate or customer. If salespeople come across as too eager, hungry and aggressive, their efforts will be fruitless, as it will be readily apparent to the other party that the relationship will be a one-sided affair.

Planning

Successful networking transcends jobs or companies. As it is something that the salesperson will benefit from throughout their entire career, wherever they go, they need to develop a long-term networking plan for the next three to five years. It takes time to properly position oneself, identify the proper contacts and nurture them into referral sources and friends.

Persistence

In addition to proper planning, effective networking takes persistence. Salespeople must have the patience to foster and develop relationships over the long haul before they can expect to see substantial results. In some cases it will take several years before a major referral source is fully developed.

In the short-term, as salespeople develop their referral sources and position themselves to take advantage of them, they will see referrals begin to slowly build. The results should be immediate, but the impact is long-term.

Commitment

If salespeople want to create and sustain a successful and effective support network, they must be committed to its success. This may include volunteer work for community groups and associations as well as other personal and professional contributions. Such efforts may take them down unexpected paths, but over the long run will pay off in results, additional customers and sales. However, without the personal commitment to its success, salespeople will quickly give up if the results aren't immediate or if it takes more time and energy than they are willing to invest.

POINTS TO PONDER – SOMETHING TO THINK ABOUT

1. Have you ever considered how essential the element of trust was in effective networking?
2. How can you take advantage of the relationships where trust and rapport are firmly established?

TRAINING ACTIVITY – APPLICATION & ACTION PLAN

1. On a sheet of paper, evaluate the following factors that can impact your efforts at effective networking:
    - Trust
    - Attitude
    - Planning
    - Persistence
    - Commitment
2. Separate the paper into two columns and list the positive and negative aspects of each factor as it applies to you.
3. Determine what can be done to maximize the positive aspects.
4. Identify how to minimize or eliminate the negatives.
5. Begin to build your networking plan based upon your analysis.

3

What Salespeople Can Expect from Networking

Many salespeople quickly abandon networking strategies when they fail to produce immediate results. In their quest for a short-term payoff, they tend to be overly aggressive and transparent in their actions. This proves to be counterproductive and undermines any possibility for success.

IMPLICATIONS – WHAT THIS MEANS TO YOU

Effective networking is a lifelong strategy. It is not a one- or two-time effort that will yield the results, but the development of a networking strategy that is incorporated into the salesperson's lifestyle. Effective networking should become part of the salesperson's persona where they naturally seek out networking opportunities in every personal and professional contact they make. They are not aggressive or pushy, only inquisitive and friendly, always understanding that the more people they know, the more opportunities there will be to foster and nurture friendships.

Many see networking as a short-term strategy where they attend events and meetings actively "working the room" for new business. Many who do this have a look of desperation that repels rather than attracts new contacts and any desire to work with them. When viewed as a lifelong strategy, salespeople aren't so aggressive and desperate.

They know that time is on their side in building friendships and fostering good will, and that this is what will reward them in the long run.

STRATEGIES, TIPS & TECHNIQUES TO APPLY

Before successful networking begins to produce results, salespeople must plan and be persistent in their efforts. However, over time, the following results can be expected:

Enhanced Visibility

Many salespeople fail because not enough companies are aware of their existence. Because they lack visibility, they do not see a sufficient number of prospects. This lack of visibility not only thwarts their prospecting efforts but also frustrates potential customers who are looking for the products and services they sell.

Effective networking over time enhances the salesperson's visibility in their marketplace. This is important because visibility provides buyers with a sense of comfort and security, allowing them to know the salesperson and how they stand out from the rest of the pack. It allows salespeople to showcase their experience as an expert and how they can provide a unique solution to resolve their problems and concerns. This allows the customer to know the salesperson is the right choice to do business with.

Improved Quality of Prospects

As the salesperson builds their network of contacts and referral sources, word gets around to prospects that they are involved in their industry and have interests suggesting they are a quality person. This helps shape a quality image of the salesperson, which is the foundation of building a relationship of mutual respect and consideration.

Contacts and referral sources also provide salespeople access to higher levels than they otherwise might have been able to make contact with. The salesperson's reputation and proven track record creates immediate credibility and provides entry. The entire selling dynamic changes: it is the prospect who wants to see the salesperson, and not the salesperson seeking to gain audience with the prospect.

Higher Levels of Interest

When salespeople are referred to a prospect, there is a very high level of probability that they will get the sale. Statistics demonstrate that 60 to 80% of referred buyers will buy from the salesperson. In these instances the salesperson's credibility is enhanced and the prospect has a high level of interest in benefiting from what the salesperson was able to do for the prospect's friend or associate's business.

Shorter Sales Cycles

Prospects referred to salespeople develop an instantaneous level of trust and rapport. They are already aware of what the salesperson is capable of doing and the results that they can expect. Because of this, the sales cycle is shortened considerably. The prospect already wants to do business; it is simply a matter of crafting an acceptable solution for them.

POINTS TO PONDER – SOMETHING TO THINK ABOUT

1. Have you viewed networking as a short-term or lifelong strategy?
2. Where have you been focusing your networking activities?

TRAINING ACTIVITY – APPLICATION & ACTION PLAN

Successful networking starts with a personal vision of long-term sales success.

1. Envision where you want to be in five to ten years.

2. Identify that types of people that you feel can help you attain your goals.
3. Identify where these types of people gather, such as civic clubs and associations.
4. Create a plan that enables you to begin to socialize and work with these individuals in civic or trade groups.
5. Determine how much time you can devote to these organizations.
6. Remember that active participation will get you known and develop a positive image and reputation that will attract these people to you and give them a desire to work with you.

4

The Ineffective Networker

There is a right way and a wrong way to network. The wrong way can be costly, time-consuming, and damaging to a salesperson's reputation. The right way takes longer, but can produce results on a number of personal and professional levels.

IMPLICATIONS – WHAT THIS MEANS TO YOU

If salespeople take the time to attend various networking events at their chamber of commerce or trade association, they will see a number of visible individuals busily "working the room" to drum up business for themselves. The same is true at meetings of various organizations. Typically, several new members will be attempting to sell and promote their products or services. To the seasoned eye, these individuals are obvious and their motives transparent.

It is important for salespeople to understand that networking involves more than these activities. In fact, individuals who use these practices to build their business actually do more harm than good by turning people off with their self-serving approach and damaging their reputations. Once created, these perceptions are often difficult to recover from.

STRATEGIES, TIPS & TECHNIQUES TO APPLY

The novice or inexperienced networker often enters into a predictable pattern. Rather than create a plan or strategy, they do what they feel is effective networking.

Flurry of Activities

The ineffective networker will start with a flurry of activities. They were probably told how effective networking is and they want to get "their piece of the pie." However, they begin with the wrong motivation: what they can gain for themselves.

Nonetheless, the salesperson will begin attending networking events at the local chamber of commerce or trade associations. They will aggressively work the room, quickly dropping one individual if they perceive them as being of no help and moving on to the next. Their conversations will be centered upon their products and how they can be of benefit to the other party. No real interaction occurs, and their motives are readily transparent.

Joins Multiple Organizations

The ineffective networker will begin to join multiple associations they feel will be of benefit, irrespective of their ability to positively contribute to the organization. Because of multiple obligations, the ineffective networker contributes nothing and develops a reputation as an individual that cannot be counted on.

Additionally, when the ineffective networker attends a meeting, they are continually pushing their products or services. Their motivation becomes obvious and transparent. Rather than becoming a contributing member of the organization and developing a reputation of care, concern and service, they make it obvious that they have joined for the business opportunity.

Becomes Pesky and Aggressive

The poor networker becomes a nuisance, aggressively contacting the people they have met at networking events or members of the organizations they have joined. Their numerous calls become obtrusive and result in a poor reputation, undermining their entire goal.

Produces Little or No Results

Due to their style of networking that repulses rather than attracts individuals, inept networkers are unable to produce results. They fail to understand why: they are doing all of the things they were told to do. But they mistake quantity for quality, thinking if joining one organization is good, joining several must be better. They do not appreciate that networking cannot be rushed, and that it takes trust and rapport to build relationships.

Quits

Ineffective networkers will quit shortly after beginning their networking efforts. Since they are incapable of getting immediate results, they see no point in continuing. Most importantly, the fact that many will have damaged their personal and professional reputations with their aggressive approach will impact them negatively in the future.

POINTS TO PONDER — SOMETHING TO THINK ABOUT

1. Have you ever had experiences with eager and ineffective networkers?
2. Have you ever used some of the techniques listed above? What happened?

TRAINING ACTIVITY — APPLICATION & ACTION PLAN

Networking involves a mutual sense of sharing and caring about others.

1. Identify your personal motivations in addition to developing new business.
2. Identify what you can offer to other individuals and organizations.
3. Determine how much time you can invest in personal networking activities.

5

Problems and Pitfalls Associated with Networking

Salespeople who are successful at networking take the time to build and foster friends and contacts. They create a sphere of influence comprised of personal and professional relationships where the goal is to help one another.

Because many salespeople fail to comprehend that this is the essence of networking, they become prone to problems and pitfalls that prevent them from being effective.

IMPLICATIONS — WHAT THIS MEANS TO YOU

Effective networking can be complex, because in creating and developing friendships and relationships, salespeople are dealing with the "human side" of selling. Successful networking hinges on the salesperson's ability to develop and foster genuine friendships and relationships first; selling becomes a secondary goal. The key is to develop a strong and substantial base of friends that can help each other. In many instances, the salesperson can help another friend by connecting him or her with another member of the network. It is a simple proposition, but once fostered and developed, it provides salespeople with a great deal of personal influence.

While salespeople often feel that someone in their network should be immediately helpful, the emphasis in networking is developing friendships and keeping them alive and vibrant. This is not done in the short-term. It takes a determined effort and focus to build relationships and make them work.

STRATEGIES, TIPS & TECHNIQUES TO APPLY

Many salespeople are mistaken as to what effective networking is and what it entails. Because of these misperceptions, they often set about networking with the following flawed approaches:

Short-Term Focus

While short-term networking efforts will yield some results for salespeople, effective networking is a long-term, if not lifetime, proposition. The common pitfall is that salespeople initiate an aggressive networking campaign, but when they fail to see immediate results or are repulsed by networking candidates, they simply quit.

Effective networking must start with a minimum of a five-year plan. This allows salespeople the time to identify and nurture contacts, get involved in helpful organizations and establish a positive image and reputation.

Lack of a Networking Plan

Like any other effective strategy, networking must be planned. When salespeople approach networking without a plan, their efforts are unfocused and fail to produce the desired outcomes and results.

An effective network plan identifies the right potential networking partners, the organizations that include these individuals and a series and sequence of goals and objectives that salespeople need to follow.

Failure to Identify the Right Contacts

Salespeople often begin to network with individuals who are not in a position to be helpful. While not to say these contacts should be ignored, it is important to target individuals with influence as key contacts. These individuals can not only connect salespeople with potential customers, but are also influential as mentors and coaches to help them grow and develop. One approach is to ask these individuals for advice and build the relationship from that point forward.

Failure to Nurture and Foster Contacts

It is common for salespeople to drop a network contact if it becomes apparent the individual will not be of immediate assistance. This makes the salesperson appear fickle and transparent.

Part of a successful networking strategy is to develop network partners as friends. If salespeople take this approach and nurture and foster friendships first, the benefits will follow. This is precisely why networking takes years to fully develop. From friendships spring trust and rapport, the essential elements for effective and successful networking.

Being Too Aggressive

Salespeople become overly aggressive because they are focused on immediate results, not the long-term impact and benefits networking can bring to them. If salespeople focus on the personal development of a relationship and nurture it, then the other aspects of networking will fall into place.

Self-Focused

One of the most common pitfalls is a self-serving focus on what the relationship can do for the salesperson. Networking implies a mutual and shared interest that is beneficial to both parties. If salespeople enter into a relationship only to take from it without giving in return, the relationship will not develop. Once the other party sees this, they will understandably feel used and terminate the relationship.

POINTS TO PONDER — SOMETHING TO THINK ABOUT

1. How many of the problems and pitfalls listed in this lesson where you aware of?
2. Have you experienced any of them? Describe the results?

TRAINING ACTIVITY — APPLICATION & ACTION PLAN

Define your existing sphere of influence. Most individuals are surprised by how large a sphere of influence they have once it is defined.

1. On a sheet of paper, begin to list your friends, associates and contacts.
2. Next to each identify their position and background.
3. Identify the key, most influential contacts.
4. Determine if there is anything you can do to further nurture key contacts.

6

The Best Networking Practices

The best networking practices are built upon trust, rapport and appreciation. Many salespeople fail to appreciate the efforts others expend on their behalf. People want to help others, but they don't want to be used or taken advantage of. The best networking practices are built upon mutual assistance and appreciation.

IMPLICATIONS – WHAT THIS MEANS TO YOU

The best networking salespeople have developed a "service attitude" toward their friends, customers and associates. Always looking for ways to be of assistance and service to others, they don't display a "what's in it for me" stance; rather their attitude is, "what can I do for you?" The difference in the two outlooks is the determining factor in their success.

When salespeople automatically look for ways to be helpful, others will automatically look for ways to reciprocate. There will be some that just take without gratitude, but the odds are in the salesperson's favor that they will receive more than they give. This isn't their motivation, but it does happen. On the other hand, when salespeople are always looking to take rather than give, they repulse others and few are willing to be helpful.

STRATEGIES, TIPS & TECHNIQUES TO APPLY

Developing active networking partners is not a difficult task, but does take time and effort.

Build Your Network

As has been stated previously, effective networking always starts with a long-term plan. Once salespeople have determined who would make ideal networking partners, they should begin by identifying the potential sources of referrals that they come into contact with. One technique is to incorporate this activity into the weekly sales plan. Once salespeople have completed the plan, they should review it to identify potential networking partners that they will be contacting during the upcoming week's activities. They should also identify existing partners that they will be contacting and plan some nurturing activities around those appointments.

Look for the Right Members

Salespeople must invest in relationships that they can sustain over long periods of time. This means identifying the right members of their network. These are individuals who can do something for them and people for whom the salesperson is able to reciprocate.

Ask Them for Their Help

Most potential networking partners are busy and focused on their own activities, and, as such, won't think about helping a salesperson unless specifically asked to do so. Most will be delighted and flattered to help the salesperson, especially if they state that they need it. Statistically, salespeople will find that approximately 90% will agree to help, but they should expect to see approximately 50% actually assist them.

Salespeople should remember that they need to close the sale for a referral in the same fashion they would close any other sale.

Be Specific About the Type of Referrals

When salespeople ask their networking partners for a referral, they should be specific about the type of referral they are seeking. They will find it is easier for someone to think of a specific name if they are thinking of a particular type of referral.

Provide Good Information

As not all members of a salesperson's network will be customers, it is important for salespeople to provide them with good information about what they can do for potential buyers. This includes how the salesperson's product can benefit a customer. Salespeople should be specific when informing a networking partner what they would like them to tell their friends about their product or service.

Give Them Something They Want in Return

The most critical element of networking is to give the networking partners something they want in return for their assistance. This is where many networking salespeople fail. They need to do favors for their networking partners, supporting them in their work and listening to their problems. Salespeople should try to feed them referrals, information and access to their contacts and anything that seems important to them. Quite often, these individuals need someone to rely on, so they are looking for the salesperson's time and friendship.

Acknowledge the Referral

Whenever a networking partner helps out, salespeople should take the time to thank him or her and relay how the contact went. If the contact results in a sale, the salesperson should send a special thank you, perhaps with a gift such as sporting or theater tickets or a dinner out. The salesperson should also clearly demonstrate their appreciation for the network partner's assistance. Most will be surprised how quickly additional referrals will follow. People have a tendency to help others, but they also want to be appreciated for their efforts.

POINTS TO PONDER — SOMETHING TO THINK ABOUT

1. Do you display a "what's in it for me" approach or a "what can I do for you" service attitude?
2. How personally appreciative are you of the help and efforts of others on your behalf? Do you feel it is expected, or are you truly appreciative?

TRAINING ACTIVITY — APPLICATION & ACTION PLAN

Determine how you can help and be of service to others.

1. Conduct a personal inventory of the things you can do, what you can offer to others and the contacts and access you can provide to them.
2. Determine how you can use your personal inventory of assets to help others.
3. Identify how you can subtly begin to be of assistance and service.

7

Developing a Networking Strategy

Networking involves getting known by the people that count, including individuals in the community, industry and areas of influence that can be helpful to the salesperson. In order to do this, salespeople must act in their self-interest by creating an effective networking strategy.

IMPLICATIONS – WHAT THIS MEANS TO YOU

Networking is important to salespeople because it creates lifelong benefits that transcend any job or employer. Concerted networking efforts impact salespeople's lives, careers and income potential. No one knows the opportunities in life that can be created by friends and contacts that are nurtured and fostered over the years.

The pursuit of effective networking activities and an operational network are essential to the sustained success of every salesperson. The most successful salespeople have built their success through the active development of networking partners and contacts who continue to feed them access to sales opportunities and new business.

STRATEGIES, TIPS & TECHNIQUES TO APPLY

Salespeople must create and implement an effective networking strategy that can be sustained over a lifetime. Since most salespeople are intensely involved in their daily sales activities and interaction with their prospects and customers, it is helpful to step back and look at networking from a strategic rather than tactical perspective. The following questions will help salespeople frame their situation and clarify where they should focus their efforts.

Formulate a Game Plan

1. Where should I focus my efforts to network right now?
2. Where should I be networking?
3. Where do my best customers and potential customers network?
4. What are three organizations I should look at getting involved in?
5. How much time should I invest in networking every week?
6. Who are five prime individuals who are ideal network partners that I want to meet?
7. What are my initial networking goals for the first year?
8. What networking skills do I possess. and which ones do I need to develop?
9. What networking tools will I need?
10. Do I know an accomplished networker that I can get advice and help from?

Networking Strategy

For some salespeople, networking can be as fearful an activity as cold calling. Rather than ask for rejection by engaging in these activities, they tend to avoid them. Networking does involve risk, but the personal fears are often unfounded. Experts have indicated that the best way to overcome these personal fears is to transform both worries and fears into goals. Additionally, the following techniques will help develop an effective networking strategy:

Small Steps – The concept of developing a personal network of contacts and referral sources can seem overwhelming. Rather than look at the entirety of the task, salespeople should take small steps. One technique is to take one action every day that advances a networking goal. Everyone is capable of doing one thing a day, and done consistently, these small actions will compound into real results.

Two Contacts a Day – Another effective technique, if performed on a consistent basis, is to call at least two people a day who can be converted into networking contacts. If salespeople make this a habit, they will contact approximately 500 people a year.

Networking Events – Whether an organization such as Rotary or Kiwanis or some other trade or civic group, salespeople should attend at least one meeting every week to make contact with other professionals.

Make Friends – As the best time to develop both friendships and potential contacts is when there is no need for the individual's help, salespeople should be making friends when they don't need something from them. As relationships strengthen and needs arise, these friends will be there to help. The request will be made on the basis of true friendship rather than solely on a personal need.

Salespeople should also make an effort to make their customers and prospects their friends as well.

Be Giving – The key to good friendships is to bring something to the relationship rather than expect to get something from it. If contacts understand the salesperson is genuine in their desire to be helpful and friendly, they will be more apt to help when the need arises.

Patience – Above all, salespeople need to practice patience. It takes a minimum of six months to develop personal relationships. If they try to force the issue, relationships will collapse. Additionally, salespeople need to remain flexible, "go with the flow," and trust their own personal judgments.

POINTS TO PONDER – SOMETHING TO THINK ABOUT

1. Does the concept of developing an effective network overwhelm you?
2. Are you worried about making new friends and contacts out of fear of rejection?

TRAINING ACTIVITY – APPLICATION & ACTION PLAN

Formulate your networking plan by answering the following questions:

1. Where should I focus my efforts to network right now?
2. Where should I be networking?
3. Where do my best customers and potential customers network?
4. What are three organizations I should look at getting involved in?
5. How much time should I invest in networking every week?
6. Who are five prime individuals who are ideal network partners that I want to meet?
7. What are my initial networking goals for the first year?
8. What networking skills do I possess and which ones do I need to develop?
9. What networking tools I will need?
10. Do I know an accomplished networker that I can get advice and help from?

8

Tracking Your Network

While it is relatively easy to keep track of several network contacts at one time, it is a nearly impossible task when a network is fully developed. As such, salespeople need a tracking system to make their contacts and keep the vital information on each contact. In this manner they are able to effectively manage and nurture the network as it grows.

IMPLICATIONS – WHAT THIS MEANS TO YOU

Many networking salespeople will organize business cards in a Rolodex or some kind of card holding file, but this is not an adequate method of fully developing the potential of a network. Effective networkers develop a full information file on each contact as well as a system allowing them to access and cross-reference information quickly and in an immediately applicable form.

It is essential for salespeople to understand that without maintaining adequate information on each active contact, their efforts to develop an effective network will fail. Information is lost or forgotten over time, leaving no way to know whom to contact when a need arises or how particular network members can be reached with helpful information. The Rolodex used to be the tool of choice and successful individuals were known by the extent of their files. Technology has simplified this process—and salespeople should take full advantage of it.

STRATEGIES, TIPS & TECHNIQUES TO APPLY

The following information should be created for each contact in the salesperson's network. While it is impractical to grill the individual about personal information, much of the information can be gleaned and observed over time. The key is for the salesperson to continually update his or her files after each contact.

Networking information can be stored in an electronic database that is cross-referenced by each individual category. While this may appear a burdensome activity when there are only a handful of contacts, when salespeople have a fully developed network over time, this is the only practical way to both manage and reference their files. If and when a contact has a need, a database search will provide salespeople with the names of other individuals who may be of assistance. They will be able to demonstrate the value of their contact by acting as the conduit between these individuals.

Networking information should include the following:

- Name, title, company
- Address, phone, fax
- Email, website
- What the company does
- What the contact does for his or her company
- Decision makers at company (each should have their own file once a relationship is established)
- Where I met him or her
- What is important to him or her?
- What can I provide to help him or her?
- How can they benefit me?
- Personal information including hobbies, interests, etc.
- Family information including spouse's and children's names, anniversaries, birthdays
- Special information including boss's name, assistant's name, partners, etc.

- Education including schools, fraternities, sororities, and extracurricular activities
- Military information including branch, rank and where stationed
- Professional affiliations including civic and professional organizations and trade groups. If an office is held, this should also be noted
- Long-range personal goals of the contact
- The top priorities of the contact
- The achievement the contact is most proud of
- Religious and political affiliations and activities
- Recreational activities
- Favorite spectator sports and teams
- Favorite conversational topics
- Favorite restaurants or clubs and meals
- Is contact primarily concerned about the opinions of others or is he or she very self-centered?
- Is the contact highly ethical?
- Strategy to develop and nurture contact
- Action sheet including contact dates and follow-up actions

POINTS TO PONDER — SOMETHING TO THINK ABOUT

1. What method do you currently use to track your network contacts?
2. Does your approach help you maximize the power of each contact?

TRAINING ACTIVITY – APPLICATION & ACTION PLAN

Develop an electronic tracking system to manage your network contacts.

1. Create a template using the information detailed above and add any other information you deem important.
2. Begin to create a file on all of your existing contacts.
3. Use a program that allows you to cross-reference and pull up files by category for easy reference.

About the Author

Timothy F. Bednarz, Ph.D. is CEO of the American Management Development Group, Inc. For over 20 years he has researched, designed and authored hundreds of learning and development programs used by Fortune 1000 companies.

He is also the author of *Great! What Makes Leaders Great. What They Did, How They Did It and What You Can Learn from It* (2011).

Speaking Availability

Timothy F. Bednarz, Ph.D. is available for speaking engagements for your next meeting or association event. He can be contacted at 800-654-4935 or by e-mail at timothy.bednarz@majorium.com.

Bulk Sales

Bulk sales of this book or any other titles available from Majorium Business Press. Inquiries can be directed to sales@majorium.com, or by phone at 800-6654-4935.

Quick Order Form

Fax orders: 715-342-1118. Send this form.

Telephone orders: Call 800-654-4935 toll-free. Have your credit card ready.

Email orders: sales@majorium.com

Postal orders: Majorium Business Press, 2025 Main Street, Stevens Point, WI 54481, USA.

Please send the following books:

____

____

____

____

Please send more FREE information on:

☐ Catalog ☐ Speaking/Seminars ☐ Mailing Lists ☐ Consulting

Name: ____________________________________

Address: ____________________________________

City: ____________________ State: _____ Zip: __________

Telephone: ____________________________________

Email address: ________________________________

Sales tax: Please add 5.5% for products shipped to Wisconsin addresses.

Shipping by air:

United States: $4.00 for first book and $2.00 for each additional product.

International: $9.00 for first book; $5.00 for each additional product (estimate).

Made in United States
Cleveland, OH
05 November 2026

47675530R00026